Animal Planet

Buggin' with Ruud

Meredith BOOKS

Des Moines, Iowa

Editor and Writer: Carrie E. Holcomb
Contributing Designer: Matthew Eberhart
Copy Chief: Terri Fredrickson
Publishing Operations Manager: Karen Schirm
Senior Editor, Asset and Information Manager: Phillip Morgan
Edit and Design Production Coordinator: Mary Lee Gavin
Editorial Assistant: Cheryl Eckert
Book Production Managers: Pam Kvitne, Marjorie J. Schenkelberg,
    Rick von Holdt, Mark Weaver
Contributing Copy Editors: Ira Lacher, Jody Speer
Category Manager, Scholastic Book Fairs: Arlene Robillard
Contributing Photographers: Ruud Kleinpaste (p. 5, 30, 43),
Philip Penketh (p. 44, 45, 47)

Meredith, Books

Executive Director, Editorial: Gregory H. Kayko
Executive Director, Design: Matt Strelecki
Managing Editor: Amy Tincher-Durik
Senior Editor/Group Manager: Jan Miller

Publisher and Editor in Chief: James D. Blume
Editorial Director: Linda Raglan Cunningham
Executive Director, New Business Development: Todd M. Davis
Executive Director, Sales: Ken Zagor
Director, Operations: George A. Susral
Director, Production: Douglas M. Johnston
Director, Marketing: Amy Nichols
Business Director: Jim Leonard

Vice President and General Manager: Douglas J. Guendel

Meredith Publishing Group

President: Jack Griffin
Executive Vice President: Bob Mate

Meredith Corporation

Chairman and Chief Executive Officer: William T. Kerr
President and Chief Operating Officer: Stephen M. Lacy

In Memoriam: E.T. Meredith III (1933-2003)

Copyright © 2005 by Meredith Corporation.
Reprinted in perfect bound tradepaper format 2007.
First Edition. All rights reserved. Manufactured and printed in China.
ISBN 978-0-696-23690-7 (perfect bound)
ISBN 0-696-23166-2 (saddle stitch)

We welcome your comments and suggestions. Write to us at:
Meredith Books, LN-120, 1716 Locust St., Des Moines, IA 50309-3023.

Special thanks to Dr. Whitney Cranshaw, Professor of Entomology,
Colorado State University, for his review of this book.

Buggin' with Ruud Book Development Team

Maureen Smith, Executive Vice President, General Manager, Animal Planet
David Doyle, Vice President, Production & Development
Mick Kaczorowski, Managing Executive Producer, Animal Planet
Sharon Bennett, Senior Vice President, Strategic Partnerships
Michael Malone, Vice President, Domestic Licensing
Carol LeBlanc, Vice President, Marketing & Retail Development
Elizabeth Bakacs, Vice President, Creative Strategic Partnerships
Jeannine Gaubert, Art Director
Christine Alvarez, Director of Publishing
Elsa Abraham, Publishing Manager
Erica Rose, Publishing Associate

Animal Planet

www.animalplanet.com
Copyright © 2005 Discovery Communications, Inc.
Animal Planet and logo are trademarks of Discovery Communications,
Inc., used under license.
All rights reserved.

Table of Contents

Meet Ruud

"Bugs," says Ruud Kleinpaste, "are incredible. They lead amazing lives that are endlessly fascinating, and let's face it, entertaining. From dazzling night light to glistening underground grottos, bugs glow, bugs dance, bugs dazzle us with breathtaking displays. They are consummate performers. It's time to put the spotlight on bugs and expose their amazing versatility and talents."

Ruud, host of the Animal Planet show *Buggin' with Ruud*, is THE Bugman. He studies bugs, plays with bugs, and appreciates all things buggy. His fascination with bugs began in college. He earned a masters of science honors degree in forestry, animal ecology, and conservation. But it soon became apparent that his true passion was the world of bugs. He became unhappy with the public's perception of bugs and soon became an ardent advocate of the good qualities of his beloved bugs.

He hosted a local talk show in New Zealand called *Ruud's Awakening*, wrote countless newspaper and magazine articles, gave lectures, and started appearing on numerous television shows—all in a pursuit to educate the public about bugs.

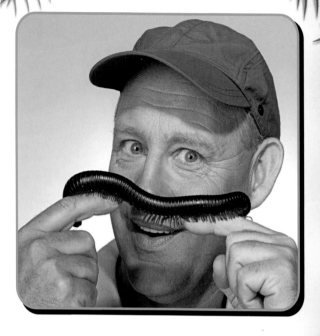

Photo courtesy Ruud Kleinpaste

Ruud's show on Animal Planet has since become a huge hit with bug fans across the country. There is nothing Ruud loves more than to teach the public about his favorite topic. His enthusiasm is contagious. Read on and see why.

It's A Bug's World

Think before you squish! Bugs make our world go 'round. Life as we know it would cease if bugs disappeared because they impact our world in so many positive ways. Bugs are some of the world's most resourceful, successful creatures. They make up more than half of all living things on this planet. They have been in existence for more than 400 million years—since way before dinosaurs roamed the Earth. How have they been able to survive that long? They are very adaptable to their environments. Some desert bugs can handle temperatures of more than 104°, while some bugs and their eggs can handle temperatures much colder than the inside of your freezer. Bugs are typically very small creatures so it doesn't take much food or water for them to survive and even thrive. Their strong and powerful exoskeletons (see below) are also keys to their survival.

Bug Fact 1

All bugs go through metamorphosis, which means the bugs change in form as they grow. In some bugs this change is very small so the adult looks much like it was as it was growing. In other cases, the adult looks nothing at all like the still-developing bug. In metamorphosis, bugs molt. This means that as they grow, they shed an outer layer of skin or exoskeleton. This allows their bodies to become bigger and bigger until they are eventually full size. Bugs normally molt 5 to 10 times in their lives.

So just what is a bug? Bugs belong to a group of animals called arthropods. All arthropods have exoskeletons. These hard, protective cases made of a material called chitin cover the bug's whole body. Bugs' muscles are attached to the underside of the exoskeleton; the pull on the plates of the exoskeleton allows the bug to move. A bug's body is divided into three main parts: head, thorax, and abdomen. All bugs have six legs, which are joined at the thorax. Those that fly typically have two or three pairs of wings, also joined to the thorax. Two antennae connected to the bug's head are used to feel, hear, and smell.

ABDOMEN

THORAX

HEAD

LEG

ANTENNAE

Bug Classification

Animals are classified into groups. The largest group is called a kingdom. The largest kingdom includes all animals, including you, your friends, your parents, your dog, and all of the bugs around you.

Kingdoms are separated into phyla. Phyla are divided into classes. Classes are divided into orders. Orders are divided into families. Families are divided into genera. Genera are divided into species.

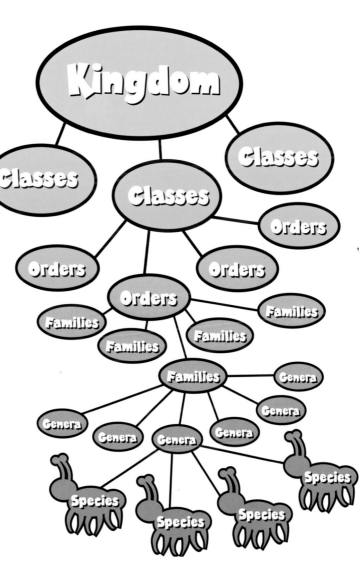

Kingdom

Classes

Classes

Classes

Orders

Orders

Orders

Orders

Families

Families

Families

Families

Families

Genera

Genera

Genera

Genera

Genera

Genera

Genera

Species

Species

Species

Species

Humans & Bees CLASSIFIED

This chart shows you how Ruud and his honeybee friend are the same in the animal kingdom, yet are different all the way down to their species.

	Human	Honeybee
Kingdom	Animal	Animal
Phylum	Chordata	Athropoda
Class	Mamalia	Insecta
Order	Primate	Hymenoptera
Family	Hominidae	Apidae
Genus	*Homo*	*Apis*
Species	*sapiens*	*mellifera*

If you're an entomologist (someone who studies bugs) or just a lover of all creatures great and small, chances are you would never harm even the smallest of insects. But for those of us who are a bit more squeamish— well, what do you think you would do if you came face-to-face with one of these bugs? Think about it. Don't worry, it's a natural reflex to automatically want to step on it, spray it, or smush it with a tissue. But what you may not know is that all bugs (even the ugly ones) are beneficial in some way. They all have good and bad qualities—just like you!

Bug Fact 3
Bugs have been living on Earth for more than 400 million years—a lot longer than humans. There are millions of species of bugs; we're not even sure exactly how many. How many human species are there? Just one. Us.

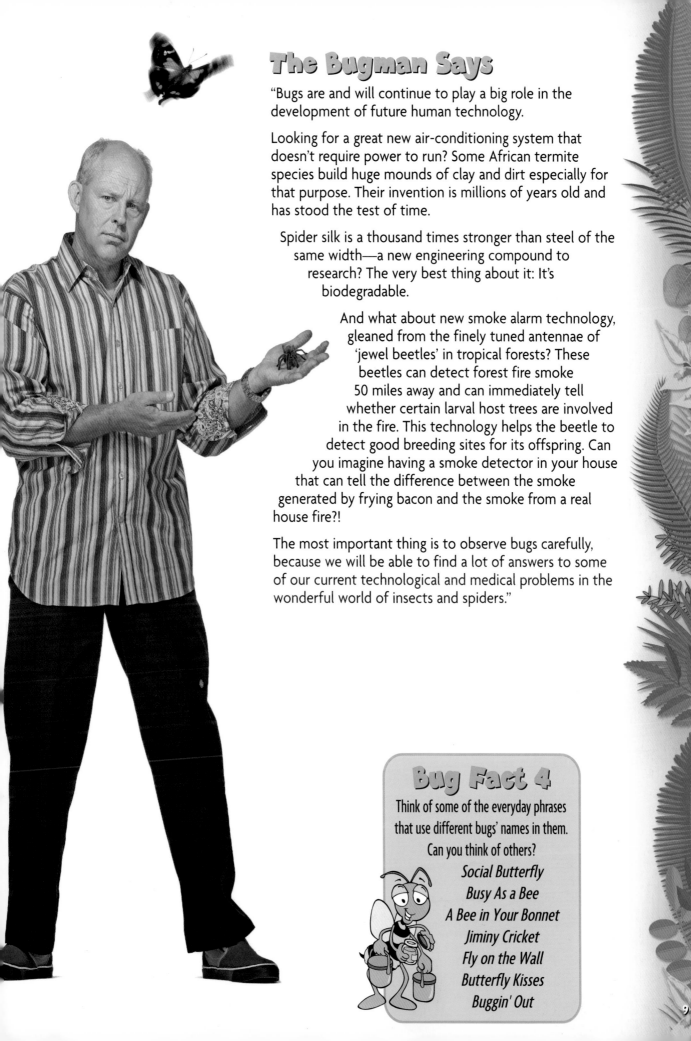

The Bugman Says

"Bugs are and will continue to play a big role in the development of future human technology.

Looking for a great new air-conditioning system that doesn't require power to run? Some African termite species build huge mounds of clay and dirt especially for that purpose. Their invention is millions of years old and has stood the test of time.

Spider silk is a thousand times stronger than steel of the same width—a new engineering compound to research? The very best thing about it: It's biodegradable.

And what about new smoke alarm technology, gleaned from the finely tuned antennae of 'jewel beetles' in tropical forests? These beetles can detect forest fire smoke 50 miles away and can immediately tell whether certain larval host trees are involved in the fire. This technology helps the beetle to detect good breeding sites for its offspring. Can you imagine having a smoke detector in your house that can tell the difference between the smoke generated by frying bacon and the smoke from a real house fire?!

The most important thing is to observe bugs carefully, because we will be able to find a lot of answers to some of our current technological and medical problems in the wonderful world of insects and spiders."

Bug Fact 4

Think of some of the everyday phrases that use different bugs' names in them. Can you think of others?

Social Butterfly
Busy As a Bee
A Bee in Your Bonnet
Jiminy Cricket
Fly on the Wall
Butterfly Kisses
Buggin' Out

Bug Puzzler #1

Test your knowledge! How much do you know about bugs?
Try to match the bug part to the bug and its description.

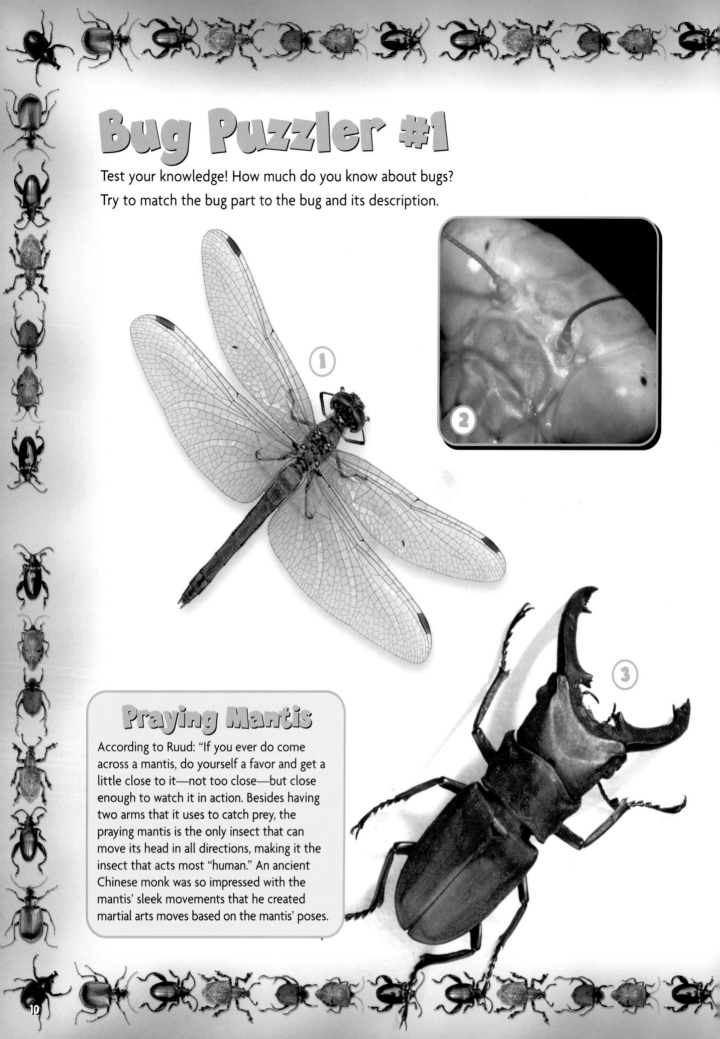

① ② ③

Praying Mantis

According to Ruud: "If you ever do come across a mantis, do yourself a favor and get a little close to it—not too close—but close enough to watch it in action. Besides having two arms that it uses to catch prey, the praying mantis is the only insect that can move its head in all directions, making it the insect that acts most "human." An ancient Chinese monk was so impressed with the mantis' sleek movements that he created martial arts moves based on the mantis' poses.

Stag Beetle
(a.k.a) Pinching Bug

These ferocious-looking bugs are named for their long, antlerlike jaws, which can sometimes be as long or longer than the bugs themselves. Their common nickname, pinching bugs, comes from their ability to bite and even draw blood from humans. Stag beetle larvae take more time than most bugs to develop into adults. In most cases the larvae live in and feed on dead and rotting wood, which is why it might take several years to mature.

Dragonfly

These colorful bugs have two sets of long, transparent wings. They are unique in the bug world because their wings can operate independently of each other, thus allowing them to fly both forward and backward at amazing speeds—up to 30 miles per hour. Experts believe dragonflies have been around for more than 300 years, and fossils suggest that they used to be as big as birds.

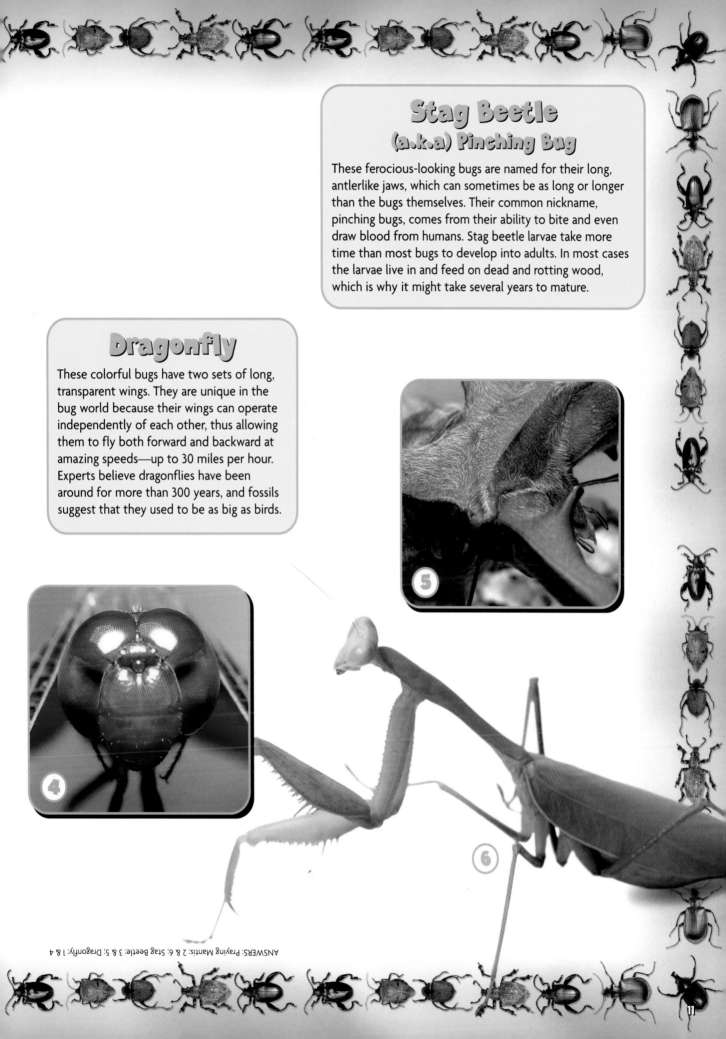

5

4

6

ANSWERS: Praying Mantis: 2 & 6; Stag Beetle: 3 & 5; Dragonfly: 1 & 4

Spiders

In reality, spiders (including tarantulas and scorpions) aren't really insects but belong to a group of animals called arachnids. There are more than 34,000 species of spiders that scientists have identified all over the world. They live pretty much everywhere from forests to freshwater and from your backyard to your house! But don't fear them! The ones in your house won't bother you and will actually do good by eating other insects that could carry diseases. Most spiders are predators, which means they hunt for their food. They release venom from their fangs, which paralyzes their prey. Then they wrap their victims in their uniquely produced silk and inject them with digestive juices to dissolve the preys' tissue. See, spiders like their meat fresh, and this time-tested method of feeding can keep the prey alive and fresh for weeks.

ABDOMEN: This softer part of the spider's body is where you'll find spinnerets, the tools for spinning webs. This organ also contains the digestive and reproductive systems of the spider.

Bug Fact 5

Some spiders are so small that we never see them. Others are monsters in comparison. The world's largest spider is the South American goliath tarantula. It can be nearly an entire foot wide!

CLAWS: These amazing claws allow spiders to cling to and walk on tough surfaces (and upside down on ceilings) and also allow them to move around their delicate webs.

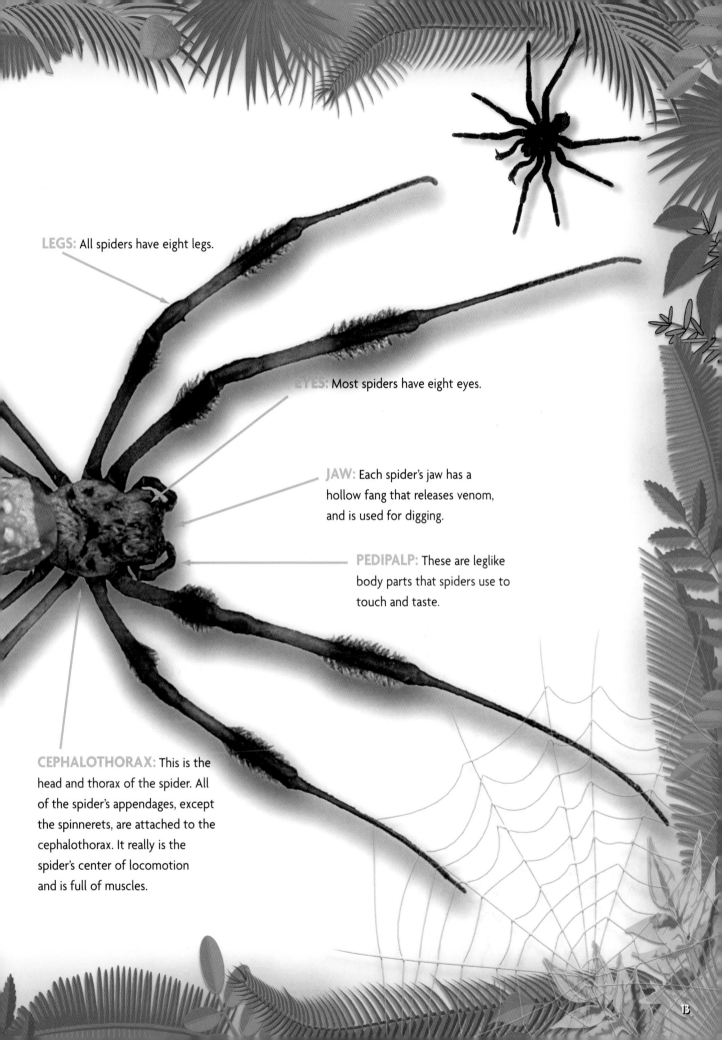

LEGS: All spiders have eight legs.

EYES: Most spiders have eight eyes.

JAW: Each spider's jaw has a hollow fang that releases venom, and is used for digging.

PEDIPALP: These are leglike body parts that spiders use to touch and taste.

CEPHALOTHORAX: This is the head and thorax of the spider. All of the spider's appendages, except the spinnerets, are attached to the cephalothorax. It really is the spider's center of locomotion and is full of muscles.

Spiders catch all sorts of creatures that may be a nuisance to us. For example, cellar spiders catch flies, mosquitoes, and other critters inside our houses. The effect spiders have on the environment is one of balance. They keep other bug populations in check and play the part of control agents.

Some spiders live on the surface of freshwater where they hunt for prey. Some of these spiders even make their webs below the water's surface. Their enemies are fish, which sometimes eat the spiders.

The Bugman Says

"Spiders can send a chill down a person's back, oh yes. But the problem that The Bugman faces is that spiders should be viewed with a great deal of respect and awe, simply because they are amazing creatures and there's much more to them than we see at first sight of those eight-legged, predators."

Bug Fact 6

Daddy longlegs aren't really spiders, even though they look like them. Most important, they don't have poison glands like spiders. Other differences? They don't make webs; have one body section, instead of two like the spider; and they have really long legs.

Spider silk has been used for centuries to help stop wounds from bleeding. Those folks were on to something, because today's scientists have discovered that the protein in spiders' webs can help stop a cut from bleeding.

Spider Facts

NUMBER OF SPECIES: More than 34,000.

HABITAT: Pretty much everywhere—from the land to the water. They live on every continent except Antarctica.

PREDATORS: Wasps, flies, other spiders, centipedes, certain reptiles, amphibians, and mammals.

DIET: Insects, small frogs, lizards, small birds, and mice.

Tarantulas

These spiders are one of the world's best known, and perhaps most feared. A tarantula's bite might be a little painful but it is really less harmful than a bee sting.

Tarantula Facts

NUMBER OF SPECIES: More than 800.

HABITAT: Underground, in rain forests, and in deserts. They are found all over the world, but are most common in South America. In the United States, they are most common in the South.

PREDATORS: Lizards, snakes, birds, and the tarantula hawk, which is a type of wasp and is the tarantula's deadliest enemy.

DIET: Insects, other arachnids, frogs, and small reptiles such as lizards and snakes.

Bug Fact 8

Jumping spiders don't make webs to catch prey. Instead, as their name implies, they jump on prey and grab it with their jaws.

Bug Fact 9

The scorpion may one day help advance medical science. Scientists are currently looking at a chemical that works like scorpion venom. Instead of hurting people it is hoped that the venom might one day help doctors who perform organ transplants or treat certain diseases such as arthritis.

Scorpions

These arachnids have been on Earth since before dinosaurs—more than 400 million years. Scorpions are typically 2 to 2½ inches long and are easily detected by a tail, which curves up and over the body.

Scorpion Facts

NUMBER OF SPECIES: More than 1,500.

HABITAT: Deserts, grasslands, forests, and caves. They are found on every continent except Antarctica. In the United States they are most common in the South.

PREDATORS: Birds, shrews, mice, bats, frogs, toads, lizards, small snakes, and other scorpions.

DIET: Insects and small rodents.

Q&A with Ruud

Ruud has some definite opinions about his favorite topic. Read on to discover some fascinating facts Ruud has learned over the years. Plus, learn his opinion on everything from his favorite bugs to how important bugs are to this world.

Q: What is so fascinating about bugs that you make your living off of them?

A: "Bugs are the driving force on this planet; without them we would not be able to live on Earth, simple as that! In fact without bugs the Earth would not exist. I have slowly become convinced that if we want to have a chance of surviving on our planet, we should first look after the bugs. They are crucial to the continued health of all life on Earth! Besides all that, bugs do all our recycling for us, they do our composting, and they provide nutrients for plants and deliver them in the right spots. Bugs help us to control pests and diseases in our crops and foods. Bugs assist us with pollination of most of our food crops. Bugs are clever examples for humans in terms of technology, locomotion, robotics, etc. Bugs provide us with all sorts of medicines, ropes, string, and materials. They make silk and honey and they provide us directly with food (you can eat bugs!). They are the key group of animals in the web of life, allowing all other animals to sustain themselves on the planet. The short answer is: That's what the show is about!"

Q: Have bugs been a lifelong fascination for you? Tell us about how and when you became interested in bugs.

A: "No, birds have. Birds have always been my number one hobby. Bugs became my hobby/passion later in life at university in Holland—at about age 21—when I met my study friend's father, who was an entomologist. He taught us about moths and butterflies, and it all started from there as a hobby. It still is a hobby! It may be good to point out that I never actually studied entomology at university at all. I tend to use that fact to inspire kids to embrace their own hobby, become the 'librarian's best friend,' and read as much as they can about their chosen interest. And when they need answers to questions, that's when you go and ask teachers for extra assistance."

Q: How and when did you get the nickname "The Bugman?"

A: "When my second son, Tristan, was born (in February 1987) I started a talk-back show on the number one radio station in New Zealand about...bugs! Because I always took the side of the bugs, I was quickly labeled 'Bugman' by the folk at the radio station and the talk-back callers in New Zealand."

Q: What is your favorite bug (or favorites) and why?

A: "Any bug with a good story to tell to kids and adults. AND SEEING THERE ARE THOUSANDS OF THOSE, it is difficult to pick one out. ALL bugs are my favorite because of their importance to this world."

Q: What is the scariest bug you've encountered?
A: "The mosquitoes and other vectors that transmit very deadly diseases from person to person."

Q: Is there anything you would like to add that the kids reading your book should know about you or about bugs?
A: "No matter what other kids say to you, if you like bugs and want to study them, go right ahead and learn as much as possible. We need good entomologists on Earth so we can save our planet from the dreadful things we are doing to it. Insects and other arthropods are the examples and the way to prevent the deterioration of our planet. After all: BUGS RUN THIS WORLD, whether we like it or not. Another thing I have noticed is that everywhere in the world, kids tend to be quite unafraid of bugs. Now, that's a great start!"

Q: What is the fastest bug?
A: "A beetle in Namibia that runs really fast over the hot sand of the desert: the *Onymacris plana*. A flat and super-streamlined black beetle. Or maybe a fast-flying hawkmoth (up to 25 miles per hour). They are great migrators over vast oceans."

Q: What is the slowest bug?
A: "Aphids are usually very slow, as they simply don't move when they sit on a plant with their long, tubular mouthparts pinned into the plant's vascular system."

Q: What is the biggest bug you have ever encountered? The smallest?
A: "Biggest: Probably the goliath bird-eating spider. Smallest: The mite that lives in the follicles of my eyelashes."

Q: Does your wife share your fascination with bugs? Your family?
A: "Yes—fascination, certainly—but not the passion. Julie is a high school teacher (English) and has her own passions and hobbies. Julie tolerates it, no problem; she won't always touch all the creepy crawlies that I find around the house, though. My son, Tristan (18 years old), is a bug boy and will assist me if I need help with bugs; he likes them too. When he was 8 or 9 years old, Tristan and I used to make kid's TV programs for New Zealand television. We were hosting the segments together and his bug knowledge is pretty good!"

Q: What is the hairiest you've encountered?
A: "A brilliant caterpillar that looked like a shaggy dog; or perhaps a velvet-hairy bird-eating tarantula spider."

Cockroaches

Cockroaches are one of the oldest bugs on Earth; fossils have been found that are more than 300 million years old. Part of the reason they have survived so long is their ability to adapt. Cockroaches have flat, oval bodies, which makes it easy for them to move through small spaces and hide in small crevices.

One type of roach, the Madagascan hissing cockroach, is famous for just what its name implies: hissing. The sounds it makes are loud enough for humans to hear. Also, if you want a bug for a pet, these roaches can be easily taken care of in homes (with an adult's supervision).

WINGS: Males have short wings while females have even shorter wings.

Cockroach Facts

NUMBER OF SPECIES: More than 4,000.

HABITAT: Just about everywhere from caves, to trees and plants to your home. They prefer dark, dank places. They live on every continent.

PREDATORS: Other cockroaches, ants, frogs, reptiles, birds, and small mammals.

DIET: Most are both meat and vegetable eaters. They mainly feast on vegetable matter, plant sap, and dead animals but they will eat many other substances such as ink or glue.

The Bugman Says

"Roaches have always been the very best recyclers in the world. They eat almost anything, anywhere and in any state of decay. Cockroaches can survive under the most appalling conditions. They adapt, survive, and are great at improvising. It makes sense that the world's very best recyclers have chosen the messiest mammal in the world as a housemate, i.e., humans. The irony is that of the 4,000 or so different species of cockroach in the world, only about 10 species can be considered as pests associated with human living quarters. All the other members of Blattodea (the order of cockroaches) live under tree bark or in damp leaf litter where they do the best job on earth of recycling dead organic matter."

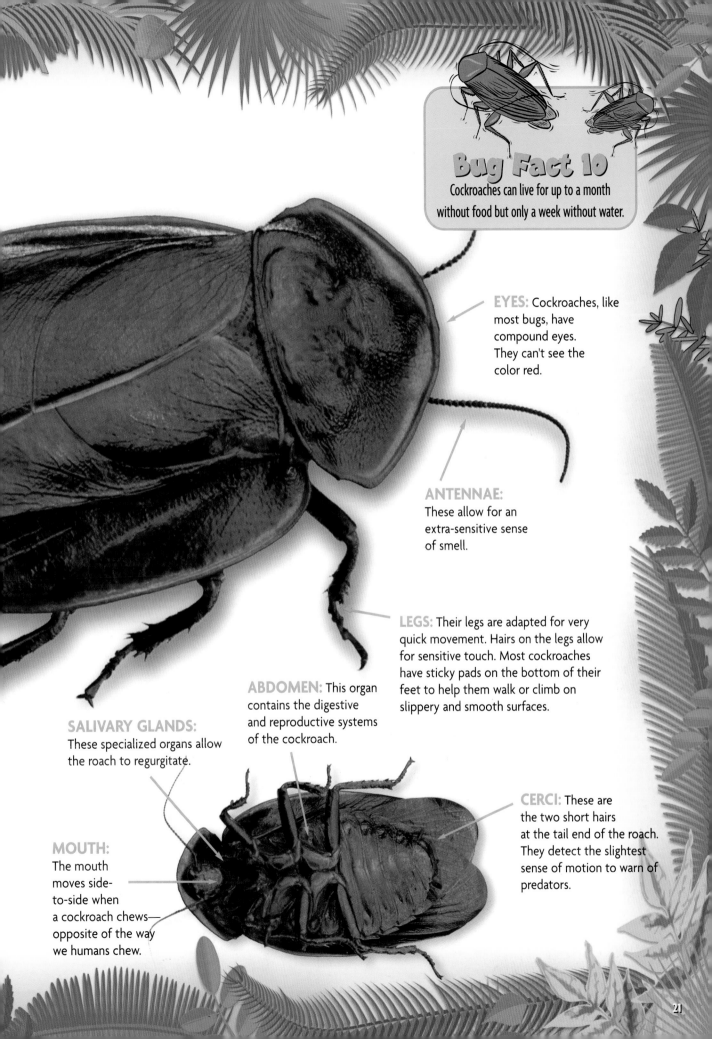

EYES: Cockroaches, like most bugs, have compound eyes. They can't see the color red.

ANTENNAE: These allow for an extra-sensitive sense of smell.

LEGS: Their legs are adapted for very quick movement. Hairs on the legs allow for sensitive touch. Most cockroaches have sticky pads on the bottom of their feet to help them walk or climb on slippery and smooth surfaces.

ABDOMEN: This organ contains the digestive and reproductive systems of the cockroach.

SALIVARY GLANDS: These specialized organs allow the roach to regurgitate.

CERCI: These are the two short hairs at the tail end of the roach. They detect the slightest sense of motion to warn of predators.

MOUTH: The mouth moves side-to-side when a cockroach chews—opposite of the way we humans chew.

Crickets

Crickets, the bugs that you see—and hear—in the summertime, are a lot like grasshoppers. Their powerful back legs give them incredible hopping power. Plus, these bugs are another insect that many people in the world eat—on purpose!

The snowy tree cricket is an old-fashioned thermometer. The song or chirp is dependent on the temperature; the tone and tempo drop with the decrease in temperature. Count the number of chirps you hear in 13 seconds, add 40, and you'll have the approximate outdoor temperature.

The Bugman Says

"Many a night you have probably lain awake while one of these insects chirps a 'lullaby.' You stumble around in the dark in hopes of finding the culprit, but, alas, never do. Before you know it, you're wishing for the death of all household crickets. So what's so great about these little symphonies anyway? Well, generally speaking, crickets are good for two things: eating and good luck. Many people enjoy eating crickets, and there are hundreds of recipes out there with crickets in the dish. Many cultures, including in the United States, believe these insects bring about good luck. Some cultures believe that stepping on a cricket will bring rain; others believe crickets bring money and hope."

ANTENNAE:
Their antennae, which are used to feel and smell, are as long as or longer than their bodies.

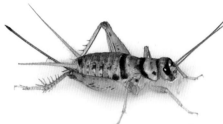

Cricket Facts

NUMBER OF SPECIES: More than 900.

HABITAT: Crickets can be found almost everywhere outside, from fields to gardens and forests. When the temperature drops, most crickets will head indoors to our homes, sheds, and businesses. They are found almost everywhere except for arctic climates.

PREDATORS: Cats, lizards, birds, wasps, small rodents, spiders, and other crickets.

DIET: Human food crumbs, pet food, and plant debris.

Bug Fact 11

In many parts of the world, people are superstitious about harming a cricket because the bugs are thought to be a sign of good luck. Some people keep crickets as pets.

MOUTH: Located under the jaw, it helps the cricket grasp food.

SPIRACLES: These series of holes located along both sides of the abdomen are used for breathing.

LEGS: Crickets' large back legs help in their ability to hop.

EYES: Like most bugs, crickets have compound eyes. The cricket also has a simple eye, which helps them distinguishes between light and dark.

CERCI: This is a pair of sensory organs located at the end of the abdomen.

OVIPOSITOR: The reproductive organ is located at the rear of the female's abdomen.

WINGS: All crickets have two sets of wings even though they can't fly; they hop, run, or walk to move about.

ABDOMEN: This organ contains the digestive and reproductive systems of the cricket.

Grasshoppers

These bugs have slender bodies and an ability to jump and leap incredible distances. In fact the grasshopper can jump more than 20 times the length of its own body. If an average adult could do that, he or she could jump nearly 40 yards! There are also grasshoppers that move by a series of short jumps. While there are many good things that grasshoppers do for our environment, they can be terribly destructive, too. A large swarm of grasshoppers can destroy an entire crop of alfalfa, clover, cotton, corn, or other grain, causing millions of dollars in crop damages every year.

WINGS: The front wing is long, narrow, and somewhat leathery. The hind wing is transparent and folds like a fan under the front wing when the grasshopper isn't flying.

Bug Fact 12

In certain parts of the world, people eat grasshoppers. In fact grasshoppers are even considered a culinary delicacy by some! Sometimes they are fried whole while other times they are ground into a paste and then fried or roasted.

LEGS: Muscles in the upper legs provide the power to jump. Their springy knees also help increase the force of the jump. Male grasshoppers also use their back legs to rub against the rough edges of the front wing; this is what causes the sounds grasshoppers use to attract mates, claim territory, and warn predators.

ANTENNAE: These are typically very long and allow the grasshopper to sense and taste.

EYES: Grasshoppers, like most bugs, have compound eyes.

SPIRACLES: These tiny holes on the grasshoppers' sides allow them to breathe.

SALIVARY GLANDS: When a grasshopper is picked up or trapped, it will spit a brown liquid. Many people call this liquid "tobacco juice."

ABDOMEN: This organ contains the digestive and reproductive systems of the grasshopper. Also, a grasshopper's ear sits in the abdominal wall.

Grasshopper Facts

NUMBER OF SPECIES: More than 20,000.

HABITAT: Fields, forests, and meadows. They are found almost everywhere except the arctic regions of the world.

PREDATORS: Wasps, mantids, toads, flies, birds, rodents, spiders, and small reptiles.

DIET: Plants, grasses, and other crops.

More Q&A with Ruud

Q: Can you tell us which *bug* is the most populous on earth?

A: "I think that has to be the springtail—a primitive insect that lives in the soil and turns organic waste into humus and plant food (a recycler!). But if you'd include bacteria in the bug group, then I'm sure the bacteria will win, hands down."

Q: Are there *bugs* that live in the water?

A: "Many different species, especially in freshwater. The health of our streams, rivers, and lakes is often measured by the communities of insects and other arthropods that live in them."

Q: How many species of *bugs* are there in the world?

A: "No one knows; best guesses are between 10 and 25 million species (we are talking arthropods here); so far, scientists have only described about a million insects!"

Q: Are there any *bugs* you are truly afraid of?

A: "I am not very trusting toward those large centipedes. They can bite without warning; they are difficult to predict or to get to know well enough to have walk over your hand! The bite is very, very painful and dangerous...don't touch them! I am also afraid of bugs that have been introduced into an area where they don't belong. When some of those exotic interlopers get established in a foreign ecosystem, the balance can become upset; that's not good for the ecosystem! They won't have any predators or parasites to keep them in check. Think of the fire ant in the southern United States, or the killer bees, or the longhorn beetles that kill trees in the eastern United States."

Q: Are there *bugs* that live in the arctic regions of the world?

A: "Many, many, many, many species! Some of the most numerous species on earth live in the arctic: Think mosquitoes in Alaska; springtails near the permafrost. Midges and tiny worms all live within the polar circle. We filmed the strangest bug of all inside the snow and ice of the Alaskan glaciers: the ice worm! It dies when temperatures are above 39°F or below 28°F! As an example: If there were no mosquitoes in the arctic, the birds wouldn't have anything to feed on, and there would be not much life around that region!"

Q: What is the worst/most painful *bug* bite or sting you have ever had?

A: "Australian bull ant—by far the worst ever! Second was the hoppy Joe ant—another Australian ant species! (what is it about those Australian ants?) Third: The bullet ant in Central and South America. Nasty and painful poisons, those ants!"

Q: Is there a bug you would actually consider to be, dare we say, ugly?

A: "No—they are fascinating and well-oiled machines, whereby all the strange bits and pieces have an important role to play in the bug's task on this world."

Q: Tell us about your fascination with butterflies? How did it get started? What is your favorite butterfly? Tell us a little more about why that is.

A: "They are just beautiful to look at. But they are also fascinating to study when you learn that each caterpillar species has very special needs and food plants; some caterpillars even live with ants to survive! And then there are the colors on the wings; no, not the colors you and I can see, but those that are only visible under ultraviolet light! These colors are probably there so males and females can recognize each other in flight! My study friend's father was a specialist in moths and butterflies; he could tell stories for hours and hours. All I had to do was listen and learn. One of my favorite butterflies is the Queen Alexandra birdwing butterfly in Papua New Guinea. It took us many days to find it and almost as long to film it. It is absolutely beautiful and huge!"

Q: How many U.S. states have you visited on your quest to study bugs?

A: "15 states so far."

Q: How many countries?

A: "About 35 countries."

Q: What do you think is the prettiest bug?

A: "The one most people find the ugliest! Example: New Zealand's weta. It is literally a large cricket with strange long hind legs and long antennae. It bites with strange, gross mandibles and kicks with its legs. Looks like a monster but I think they are extremely pretty. A closely related American insect is the lubber grasshopper in the Eastern United States."

Q: What is the smelliest bug?

A: "The proverbial stinkbug. These creatures seem to occur all over the world, and they all do the same thing: smell bad so predators won't eat them. Mind you, often that same smell is a warning system to their brothers and sisters that a predator is lurking nearby. Often the warned bugs then 'drop dead' to the ground and 'play possum' to avoid detection!"

Q: How many times do you estimate you have been bitten or stung by a bug?

A: "Thousands of times."

Q: Have you ever been sick or been to the hospital because of a bug bite or sting?

A: "Not yet—I suppose I have been lucky!"

Beetles

Beetles are so adaptable that they might just be the most prosperous bugs on Earth. There are more species of beetles in the world than any other kind of animal, and scientists are discovering more all the time. Beetles have been on Earth for millions of years. Some species have maintained the same structure over the years, while others have evolved into strange shapes to suit their surroundings. Beetles also vary in size from those barely visible to those that can be up to 8 inches long. One common feature of all beetles, despite their size, is hard, rigid front wings that fit over back wings. This prevents the back wings from becoming damaged and makes it easier for beetles to search for food because it allows them to get into places most other bugs cannot.

Those red, yellow, pink, or orange ladybugs that we all think are so cute are actually kinds of beetles. The bright colors of adult ladybugs warn predators that they taste horrible. When disturbed, they secrete a smelly fluid from their joints, which can cause a stain. This is called reflex-bleeding.

Beetle Facts

NUMBER OF SPECIES: More than 400,000.

HABITAT: Deep in the ground, under rocks, in mud, in decaying plant and animal matter, in water, in the desert, or in bird and mammal nests. They live on every continent.

PREDATORS: Other beetles.

DIET: Many are vegetarians, while others are predators that feed on other animals or decaying animals. Some eat aphids, scale insects, and other soft-bodied bugs.

The Bugman Says

"Carpet beetles aim for our woolen fabrics and furnishings. They're just doing what comes naturally. They were born to recycle the fur, feathers and even skins of dead animals. Have you ever tried to eat wool? The reality is you can't, simply because wool is made of keratin, a large and long molecule that is hard to break down. There are very few animals that can actually digest and break down keratin, and carpet beetles are some of those specialists. So, when those insects fly into your living room and spy the carpet on the floor, their natural reaction is, 'Don't worry about a thing! I'll clean all that dead sheep wool up in no time!' After all, they've been doing that sort of thing now for many millions of years."

ANTENNAE: Beetles have many types of antennae: clubbed, sawtoothed, featherlike, or combed. They use their antennae to locate food and mates.

HEAD: In addition to the eyes, the head also has mouthparts that allow biting and chewing, with well-developed jaws, or mandibles. The mandibles in some beetles are very large and can even resemble deer antlers.

LEGS: All beetles have six legs. Some have modified hind legs for jumping, while others have sharp spines on their legs used to defend themselves.

EYES: Beetles, like most bugs, have compound eyes.

TARSI: Each of the beetle's six legs has a series of small segments at the ends tipped with claws. This helps them hold tightly to tree trunks or other surfaces.

PRONOTUM: The area above the elytra, which is part of the thorax.

ABDOMEN: This organ contains the digestive and reproductive systems of the beetle.

Bug Fact 18

You know those bugs that you see at night and love to catch in glass jars? You might know them as lightning bugs. They are actually a type of beetle called a firefly. These beetles have a special organ at the tip of their abdomen that emits flashes of green or yellow light. The main function of this light is to attract a mate. The firefly is one of the few bugs that can emit light from its own body.

WINGS: Beetles have two sets of wings. The hard front wings are called elytra, which serve to protect the soft hind wings that are used for flying.

Flies

Most flying bugs have four wings; flies have two. The flies you are probably most familiar with are the ones that sneak into your house when you open the door or invade your outdoor picnic.

Flies have to suck up their food because they can't chew. Their food has to be in a liquid form for them to eat it, so their tongues act as a sponge to slurp up their food. When a house fly lands on food, it throws up on the food. The digestive juices, enzymes, and saliva in the vomit begin to break down the food. The fly can then suck up the liquid food. If flies eat food from garbage cans or any other source of germy food, some of those germs stick to the fly, and when it vomits on its next snack—your lunch, perhaps—it can transfer those germs. Some flies (such as mosquitoes) can bite and suck blood. When you do get bitten, it is typically a female because she needs the protein from your blood for the development of her eggs.

Bug Fact 14

Each of a fly's compound eyes consists of as many as 4,000 ommatida. Each of these tiny units works like a miniature eye and sees just a bit of the big picture. Flies can't produce a terribly sharp image, but they can sense movement very well.

Photo courtesy Ruud Kleinpaste

The Bugman Says

"Stable flies are one of the nastiest uninvited houseguests you'll ever find. They are widespread throughout America, but in the southern states they can reach plague proportions. Stable flies are diabolically wicked. They drink our blood. Stable flies are known as pool feeders. Most other blood-sucking insects are quite surgical in the way they extract a meal, but stable flies rip and tear their way though skin, creating pools of blood and causing plenty of pain."

Fly Facts

NUMBER OF SPECIES: More than 120,000.

HABITAT: On or near the animals or humans on which they feed. Near decaying vegetation and fruit. They live on every continent.

PREDATORS: Humans with fly swatters, other flies, birds, and spiders.

DIET: Human food, garbage, manure, blood.

ABDOMEN: This organ contains the digestive and reproductive systems of the fly.

HEAD: In addition to the eyes, the head also has mouthparts that are adapted to feeding methods such as sucking, chewing, stabbing, and biting.

ANTENNAE: Usually very small in flies, these are used to smell, touch, and hear.

HALTERES: These are modified remnants of back wings that help flies to balance.

SPIRACLES: Flies breathe through these special openings on their sides.

MOUTH: These are a sponge-like appendage that can mop up liquids.

LEGS: All flies have six legs. Fine hairs on their legs help them taste. They are able to walk easily on any surface because their feet are structured like suction cups.

EYES: Flies, like most bugs, have compound eyes.

Bug Puzzler #2

Test your knowledge! How much do you know about bugs?
Try to match the bug part to the bug and its description.

1

2

Dung Beetle

According to Ruud: "Dung beetles lay their eggs inside poop, because it's a perfect environment for their larvae to grow in. It may look revolting but these beetles compete fiercely to get at the dung. They wait high in the tree foliage for fresh deposits from the monkeys above. Once the beetle has the dung, it's rolled into a ball. But what comes next would impress a top circus trapeze artist. Riding its precious cargo all the way down, the beetle drops about ten stories to the forest floor below. So what's the beetle's secret? Well, compared to us, the bug has a much larger surface size for its weight. So its body acts like kind of a parachute, allowing it to approach the ground at much reduced speed."

3

Millipede

According to Ruud: "The millipede is a slow moving creature you're likely to find outside your house in a damp area: under leafs, flower pots, and compost. Millipede is Latin for 1,000, but, biologically speaking, millipedes have from 47 to 197 pairs of legs. Millipedes are brown or black and their bodies are made up of two parts: a head and segmented trunk. Two pairs of legs are attached to each body segment. If you do see a millipede in the garage or basement, don't worry, they do not bite or sting. Millipedes are nocturnal which means they're active at night, rather than during the day. "

④

Walking Stick

These slender bugs get their name from their appearance; they look just like leafless sticks. This gives them a great defense system. If they are threatened they can camouflage themselves from their predators. Walking sticks are the only bug that can regenerate lost limbs. If a leg is cut off, a new one grows in its place—kind of like a starfish.

⑤

⑥

Bees

Bees are one of the most well-known and perhaps most-feared bugs. This fear factor is something bug experts want people to change. Bees usually leave people alone and typically only sting when they or their hives are in danger. They are, however, attracted to certain soaps, lotions, and hairsprays. If they come near you, they are probably just confused. The best thing to do if a bee does come close to you is to stand still. We know this is hard, but sudden motion will make them feel that they are in danger and this is when they might sting. And while a sting might hurt, it won't have any lasting effects unless you are allergic to bee stings. Once a bee stings you, the jagged stinger tears out of the bee's abdomen, along with the poison gland. This kills the bee. So it is best for all involved to avoid stings.

Honeybees are the only bug to produce food for humans, which is, of course, honey. The color and flavor of the honey depends on what types of flowers the bees visit to collect nectar. Honeybees visit about 2 million flowers to make 1 pound of honey.

Bug Fact 15

Bees communicate through a complex dance. This communicates direction and distance from the hive to nectar sources. This is known as the "bee dance language."

EYES: Like most bugs, bees have compound eyes. They can't see the color red, but can see ultraviolet light, which is invisible to us.

HEAD: Bees' mouths have long tongues suited for gathering nectar from flowers.

Bee Facts

NUMBER OF SPECIES: More than 20,000.

HABITAT: Some live in nests called hives, while others live alone. The hive is ruled by a queen bee. She is the largest bee in the hive, and she is the only female to mate. The worker bees do all of the work both inside and outside the hive and all are females. Their jobs include caring for larvae, making wax, building honeycomb, cleaning up the hive, storing pollen, making honey, guarding the hive, and collecting pollen and nectar. The male bees, called drones, that live in the hives are there for mating only. Bees live on all continents except in the arctic. However, some bumblebees can survive as far north as the polar tundra.

PREDATORS: Wasps, mites, small mammals, badgers, skunks and bears. However, most predators avoid them because of their sting.

DIET: Royal jelly, which is a paste made by worker bees, and pollen and nectar collected from flowers and honey. The queen bee eats only royal jelly, .

The Bugman Says

"As most people know, the whole process of pollination allows pollen to be spread from flower to flower, causing genetic material to become distributed and fruits or seeds to set on the plant. It literally is the way plants reproduce; therefore, pollinators need to be kept 'happy' by the plant, for without those pollinators the plant species will not reproduce, have offspring, and hence be doomed. Without these vital pollinators we would have no fruit, nuts, wine, or cider, as well as many species of flowering plants and timber trees—hard to imagine!"

ABDOMEN: This organ contains the digestive and reproductive systems of the bee and wasp. It also contains a venom gland, which is attached to the bug's stinger.

PEDICEL: The waist or constriction between the base of the abdomen and thorax.

LEGS: These contain the pollen basket, which the bee uses to store pollen it collects from flowers. Females have brushes on their legs. They use them to remove pollen that sticks to these body hairs.

Wasps

Wasps are a lot like bees. Their anatomy is similar, and the way they live is similar. There are some differences between the two. Unlike bees, who die after one sting, wasps can sting over and over again. This is because their stinger is straight and pulls right back out after stinging. Many species of wasps are called parasitic. This means that they live as parasites inside other insects. This is good for the environment because it helps eliminate many insects that cause damage.

Bug Fact 16

NEVER squish a yellowjacket within 15 feet of its nest. This type of wasp may release a special scent, its alarm pheromone. Within seconds the other wasps in the nest will descend and come to the victim's aid—and this aid probably includes stinging you.

Wasp Facts

NUMBER OF SPECIES: More than 25,000.

HABITAT: Some live in huge colonies, while others live alone. As with bees, each colony has a queen bee, worker bees, and drones.

PREDATORS: Army ants and other wasps.

DIET: Fruit, nectar, plants, and plant sap. Larvae feed on insects.

OTHER COMMON WASPS: Hornet, paper wasp, parasitic wasp, velvet ant, and mud dauber.

Bug Fact 17

Hornets are a type of wasp known for their painful sting and ferocious disposition. Hornets are the biggest wasp and make the biggest nests. The nests can be up to 50 inches long and 40 inches around—bigger than a basketball!

Ants

Entomologists believe that ants evolved from wasps millions of years ago. Ants are one of the world's most successful creatures; they are intelligent insects. A study once showed that an ant's brain can function as quickly as a computer.

Ants spray their predators with formic acid (a colorless, stinky liquid) to defend themselves. Some birds let ants crawl on their bodies and spray them with this acid. This process, called anting, gets rid of parasites from the birds' feathers.

Bug Fact 18

Ants can run very quickly because they have very strong legs. If a human could run as fast for his or her size as an ant, he or she could run as fast as a racehorse.

The Bugman Says

"Ants are often thought of as a real nuisance. These creatures gather their food in your garden or even your house—it all depends on what type of food they feed on and what you provide them with. Some species feed on protein debris, thereby cleaning the Earth of miscellaneous dead insects and other animals, so those bodies don't lie around for years and years. Of course, spilled bits of cat and dog food are just as much part of their diet. Other ants have a sweet tooth and go for nectar, honeydew, and overripe fruit. They clean that up everywhere. If you spill some jam or honey in the kitchen, these ants will show no hesitation doing what they've been doing for millions of years: march in and get rid of it. Just leave a jar of sugar open and you'll know exactly what I mean."

METASOMA: This is the poison sac of the ant. Many types of ants have stingers that are used for protection against predators.

Ant Facts

NUMBER OF SPECIES: More than 20,000.

HABITAT: Most live in very large colonies or anthills; ants are very social insects. Others nest in trees. Ants live on every continent.

PREDATORS: Toads, lizards, other ants and insects, bats, and birds.

DIET: Dead insects and animals, melons and overripe fruit, jams, honey, seeds, oils, and sugar.

EYES: Ants, like most bugs, have compound eyes.

SPIRACLES: Ants breathe through these special openings on their sides.

HEAD: Ants communicate with their antennae, which bend at distinctive angles that make them look like tiny elbows. They also use their antennae for tasting, smelling, and feeling. The head also has two strong pinchers that carry food, dig, and defend. Just inside the mouth is a small pocket where ants can store food. They can give this food to other ants.

THORAX: This is the middle section of the ant, where all the legs are attached. Each leg has a sharp claw at the end to help the ant climb and hang onto objects and surfaces.

WINGS: Some ants have two sets of wings. The first pair is much larger than the hind pair.

Butterflies
Ruud's Passion

Of all of the bugs in the world, Ruud is probably the most passionate about butterflies. The father of one of his college friends was an entomologist who taught Ruud all about butterflies. Ruud says this is how he began his hobby of studying the bug world—and even now, when he makes his living off bugs, he still calls it a hobby. How could something someone loves so much be called "work?"

COMPLETE METAMORPHOSIS

All butterflies go through a process called complete metamorphosis to become an adult. This means they go through four stages of life: egg, larva (caterpillar), pupa (chrysalis), and adult (butterfly). Depending on the species, each stage is different and takes a different amount of time—from a month to a year. The larva or caterpillar stage is the main stage for growth. During this period the larva eats and eats until its skin literally falls off because it no longer fits its body. This is called molting, which the larva will do four to six times before emerging as a butterfly.

EYES: Butterflies, like most bugs, have compound eyes.

ANTENNAE: Butterflies use this clublike body part to smell.

PROBOSCIS: The strawlike structure mouthpart allows them to suck up food. They have no mouth or teeth to chew their food.

WINGS: The butterfly's wings are covered with minuscule scales that are arranged in precise patterns, which gives the insect its beautiful colors.

SPIRACLES: Small holes on the abdomen allow the butterfly to breathe.

LEGS: Most butterflies have six legs. Caterpillars have six legs like other insects along with four to ten prolegs that distinguish them as larvae of butterflies. These prolegs disappear in the adult butterfly. Butterflies use the bottom of their feet to taste.

ABDOMEN: This organ contains the digestive and reproductive systems of the butterfly.

Butterfly Facts

NUMBER OF SPECIES: More than 20,000.

HABITAT: Meadows, marshes, swamps. gardens, orchards. They live on all continents except Antarctica.

PREDATORS: Birds, lizards, bats—though many predators learn to avoid butterflies by their bright and vivid colors, which signals a very unpleasant taste.

DIET: Animal waste, nectar, rotting fruit, leaves, seeds, tree sap, and thistle.

Bug Fact 20

How do you tell a butterfly from a moth? Moths don't have the telltale knobs at the end of their antennae like butterflies do. Also, butterflies tend to have vibrantly colored wings, whereas moths tend to be very drab in color.

Butterflies range drastically in size from a tiny ⅛ inch to a huge almost 12 inches across. Female Queen Alexandra's birdwing butterflies are the largest in the world. Pygmy blues are the smallest.

Photo courtesy Ruud Kleinpaste

Bug Fact 21

Butterflies lay their eggs on plants so that when the eggs hatch, the caterpillar that emerges has immediate access to food: the plant on which it was born.

The Bugman Says

"Some of the brightest-colored butterflies can be the most poisonous ones! They obtain this poison in the caterpillar stage while feeding on toxic plants. The poisons are passed on, via the chrysalis, to the butterfly for protection from predators. Birds recognize the bright warning colors and won't even think about touching these butterflies."

True Bugs

Most people use the word "bug" to refer to any type of insect. In reality true bugs are those with strawlike mouthparts that pierce and suck fluids from plants and animals. Most true bugs have two pairs of wings and the front wing is unusual; it is half thick and half thin, meaning Hemiptera or half-winged insects. Many scientists say this order is one of the most destructive in the bug world.

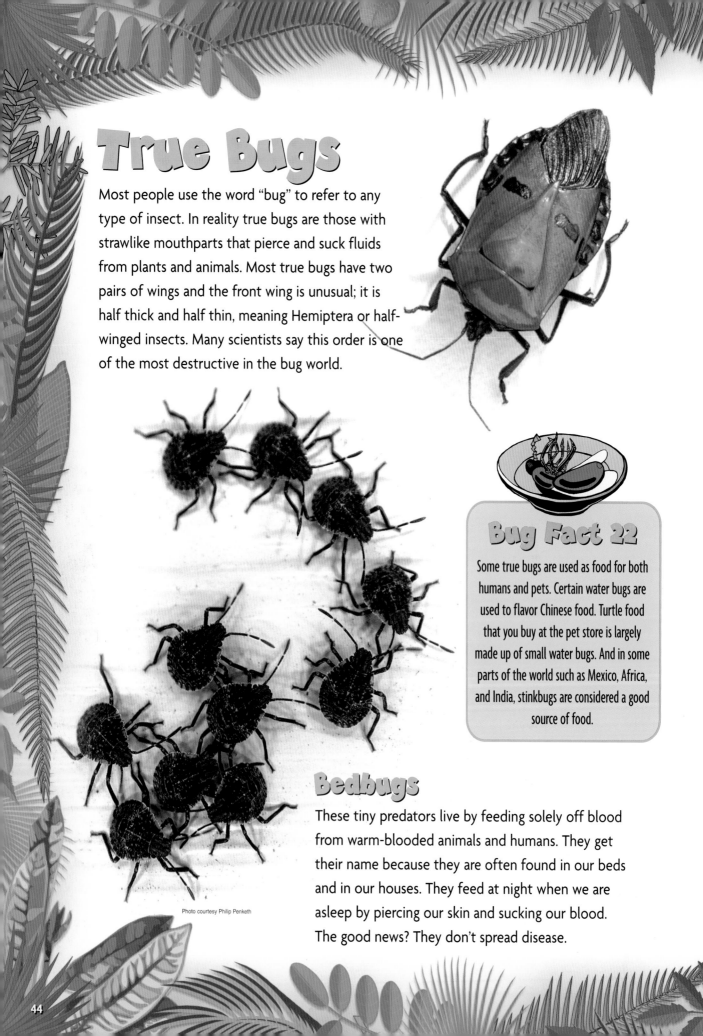

Photo courtesy Philip Penketh

Bug Fact 22

Some true bugs are used as food for both humans and pets. Certain water bugs are used to flavor Chinese food. Turtle food that you buy at the pet store is largely made up of small water bugs. And in some parts of the world such as Mexico, Africa, and India, stinkbugs are considered a good source of food.

Bedbugs

These tiny predators live by feeding solely off blood from warm-blooded animals and humans. They get their name because they are often found in our beds and in our houses. They feed at night when we are asleep by piercing our skin and sucking our blood. The good news? They don't spread disease.

Photo courtesy Philip Penketh

Photo courtesy Philip Penketh

Ambush Bugs

These stealthy critters sit very still on or near flowers. They have amazing camouflage, which allows them to remain undetected while an unwitting creature happens by to gather nectar.

True Bug Facts

NUMBER OF SPECIES: More than 82,000.

HABITAT: This varies greatly from bug to bug, but many live in the water.

PREDATORS: Other bugs, birds, small rodents, and small mammals.

DIET: Other bugs, small animals, worms, and tadpoles.

Giant Water Bugs

The Bugman says, "This clever critter has a built-in snorkel, a siphon tube on its rear end that draws in air. How cool is that? A snorkel in your butt!"

Water Striders

These are one of very few bugs that can survive in the ocean's saltwater. They also live in freshwater ponds and slow-moving streams. They rarely go under the water but rather float or walk on water. Because of this ability they are sometimes called "Jesus bugs."

Assassin Bugs

These bugs are so named because they lie in wait for their unassuming victims. They are very aggressive and aren't afraid to attack creatures bigger than they, including humans.

Photo courtesy Philip Penketh

Stinkbugs

Want some easy advice? Don't mess with a stinkbug or you will end up stinky. These bugs have glands that secrete a terrible odor when they are disturbed.

Glossary

ANTING: The deliberate placing of ants or other bugs on birds' feathers.

ARACHNIDS: A member of a large group of arthropods, including spiders and scorpions.

ARTHROPODS: Any animal with a hard exoskeleton and jointed legs.

ANTENNAE: The slender, movable body parts on the heads of bugs that are used like our sensory organs.

CATERPILLAR: The wormlike larva of a butterfly.

CEPHALOTHORAX: The front region of a spider's body that is a fusion between the head and thorax.

CHITIN: The substance that forms part of the hard outer body of a bug.

CHRYSALIS: The pupa stage of certain bugs' development.

CLASS: A major category in biological classification that is above the order and below the phylum.

COCOON: A silky case formed by an insect larva in order to pupate.

DRONE: A male bee.

EXOSKELETON: A hard skin that acts as an external supportive covering.

FAMILY: A group of related plants or animals ranking in biological classification above a genus and below an order.

FORMIC ACID: A colorless strong-smelling acid produced in some insects that irritates the skin and is often used in defense.

GENUS: A category of classification in biology that ranks above the species and below the family, contains related species, and is named by a capitalized Latin noun.

HALTERE: A pair of club-shaped organs that are the modified hind wings of a two-winged fly. They serve to maintain perfect balance and agility in flight.

HEAD: The upper or front part of a bug's body that contains the brain, the chief sense organs, and the mouth.

INSECTA: A class of Arthropoda.

LARVA: An immature stage of an arthropod.

MOLT: To shed a layer of skin.

NOCTURNAL: Active at night.

OMMATIDIA: One of the elements or facets that make up the compound eye of an arthropod.

ORDER: A category of biological classification ranking above the family and below the class.

PEDIPALP: One of the second pair of organs that lie on each side of the mouth in spiders and other insects that are used for eating and handling food. Spiders use them to mate as well.

PHYLUM: One of the main categories in biological classification ranking above the class and below the kingdom.

POLLINATE: To apply pollen to a flower or plant.

PREDATOR: An animal that eats bugs or other animals to survive.

PUPA: In complete metamorphosis the stage between larva and adult.

SPECIES: A category of living things that ranks below a genus, is made up of related individuals able to produce fertile offspring, and is identified by a two-part scientific name.

SPINNERET: An organ for producing threads of silk from the secretion of the silk glands.

SPIRACLE: A hole in the exoskeleton that leads into a bug's breathing tube.

STRIDULATION: A usually high-pitched creaking or musical sound made by many insects such as grasshoppers, katydids, and crickets. The sound is produced by rubbing together wings, legs, or specially modified body parts.

TARSI: The part of the limb of a bug that corresponds to our hands or feet.

THORAX: The middle region of a bug's body to which the legs and wings are attached.

VECTOR: An organism that can pass diseases from one host to another.

VENOM: The poisonous matter that bugs secrete primarily for catching prey or for their own defense.

VERTEBRATE: An animal with a backbone.